The Ancient Hanged Poems Of The Arabs

Charles F. Horne

Kessinger Publishing's Rare Reprints

Thousands of Scarce and Hard-to-Find Books
on These and other Subjects!

- Americana
- Ancient Mysteries
- Animals
- Anthropology
- Architecture
- Arts
- Astrology
- Bibliographies
- Biographies & Memoirs
- Body, Mind & Spirit
- Business & Investing
- Children & Young Adult
- Collectibles
- Comparative Religions
- Crafts & Hobbies
- Earth Sciences
- Education
- Ephemera
- Fiction
- Folklore
- Geography
- Health & Diet
- History
- Hobbies & Leisure
- Humor
- Illustrated Books
- Language & Culture
- Law
- Life Sciences

- Literature
- Medicine & Pharmacy
- Metaphysical
- Music
- Mystery & Crime
- Mythology
- Natural History
- Outdoor & Nature
- Philosophy
- Poetry
- Political Science
- Science
- Psychiatry & Psychology
- Reference
- Religion & Spiritualism
- Rhetoric
- Sacred Books
- Science Fiction
- Science & Technology
- Self-Help
- Social Sciences
- Symbolism
- Theatre & Drama
- Theology
- Travel & Explorations
- War & Military
- Women
- Yoga
- *Plus Much More!*

We kindly invite you to view our catalog list at:
http://www.kessinger.net

THE HANGED POEMS

" They stand at the summit of the eminence of old Arabic literature."

— FAIZ-ULLAH-BHAI.

THE HANGED POEMS

THE POEM OF IMRU-UL-QUAIS [1]

Stop, oh my friends, let us pause to weep over the remembrance of my beloved.
Here was her abode on the edge of the sandy desert between Dakhool and Howmal.

The traces of her encampment are not wholly obliterated even now;
For when the South wind blows the sand over them the North wind sweeps it away.

The courtyards and enclosures of the old home have become desolate;
The dung of the wild deer lies there thick as the seeds of pepper.

On the morning of our separation it was as if I stood in the gardens of our tribe,
Amid the acacia-shrubs where my eyes were blinded with tears by the smart from the bursting pods of colocynth.

As I lament thus in the place made desolate, my friends stop their camels;
They cry to me "Do not die of grief; bear this sorrow patiently."

Nay, the cure of my sorrow must come from gushing tears.
Yet, is there any hope that this desolation can bring me solace?

[1] This is supposed to be the oldest of the "hanged" poems. Like the others it shifts abruptly from theme to theme, and is full of poetic comparisons. Indeed, its author is said to have started this fashion, winning for himself the name of "The creator of images."

So, before ever I met Unaizah, did I mourn for two others;
My fate had been the same with Ummul-Huwairith and her
neighbor Ummul-Rahab in Masal.

Fair were they also, diffusing the odor of musk as they moved,
Like the soft zephyr bringing with it the scent of the clove.

Thus the tears flowed down on my breast, remembering days
of love;
The tears wetted even my sword-belt, so tender was my love.

Behold how many pleasant days have I spent with fair
women;
Especially do I remember the day at the pool of Darat-i-
Juljul.[2]

On that day I killed my riding camel for food for the
maidens:
How merry was their dividing my camel's trappings to be car-
ried on their camels.

It is a wonder, a riddle, that the camel being saddled was yet
unsaddled!
A wonder also was the slaughterer, so heedless of self in his
costly gift!

Then the maidens commenced throwing the camel's flesh into
the kettle;

[2] The poet in this and the following lines refers to an incident which
is thus told us: during his wooing of Unaizah he followed her and the
other maidens when they rode on camels to the pool Darat-i-Juljul. The
women bathed in the pool and he captured their clothes and would not
surrender these until each one came out of the water in turn and asked
for hers. They held back so long before they yielded to this, that afterward they complained of being faint with hunger. Thereon he lavishly
slew his camel so they could have it immediately for food. When they
had eaten, they would not leave him stranded in the desert, so divided
the trappings of his camel, each carrying home a part upon her beast,
while the carrying of the poet himself fell to Unaizah. She jestingly
protested that the howdah on her camel's back was too small for them
both.

The fat was woven with the lean like loose fringes of white twisted silk.

On that day I entered the howdah, the camel's howdah of Unaizah!
And she protested, saying, " Woe to you, you will force me to travel on foot."

She repulsed me, while the howdah was swaying with us;
She said, " You are galling my camel, Oh Imru-ul-Quais, so dismount."

Then I said, " Drive him on! Let his reins go loose, while you turn to me.
Think not of the camel and our weight on him. Let us be happy.

" Many a beautiful woman like you, Oh Unaizah, have I visited at night;
I have won her thought to me, even from her children have I won her."

There was another day when I walked with her behind the sandhills,
But she put aside my entreaties and swore an oath of virginity.

Oh, Unaizah, gently, put aside some of this coquetry.
If you have, indeed, made up your mind to cut off friendship with me, then do it kindly or gently.

Has anything deceived you about me, that your love is killing me,
And that verily as often as you order my heart, it will do what you order?

And if any one of my habits has caused you annoyance,
Then put away my heart from your heart, and it will be put away.

And your two eyes do not flow with tears, except to strike me
    with arrows in my broken heart.
Many a fair one, whose tent can not be sought by others, have
    I enjoyed playing with.

I passed by the sentries on watch near her, and a people desir-
    ous of killing me;
If they could conceal my murder, being unable to assail me
    openly.

I passed by these people at a time, when the Pleiades appeared
    in the heavens,
As the appearance of the gems in the spaces in the ornamented
    girdle, set with pearls and gems.

Then she said to me, " I swear by God; you have no excuse
    for your wild life;
I can not expect that your erring habits will ever be removed
    from your nature."

I went out with her; she walking, and drawing behind us,
    over our footmarks,
The skirts of an embroidered woolen garment, to erase the
    footprints.

Then when we had crossed the enclosure of the tribe,
The middle of the open plain, with its sandy undulations and
    sandhills, we sought.

I drew the tow side-locks of her head toward me; and she
    leant toward me;
She was slender of waist, and full in the ankle.

Thin-waisted, white-skinned, slender of body,
Her breast shining polished like a mirror.

In complexion she is like the first egg of the ostrich — white,
    mixed with yellow.

Pure water, unsullied by the descent of many people in it, has
nourished her.

She turns away, and shows her smooth cheek, forbidding with
a glancing eye,
Like that of a wild animal, with young, in the desert of
Wajrah.

And she shows a neck like the neck of a white deer;
It is neither disproportionate when she raises it, nor unorna-
mented.

And a perfect head of hair which, when loosened, adorns her
back,
Black, very dark-colored, thick like a date-cluster on a heavily
laden date-tree.

Her curls creep upward to the top of her head;
And the plaits are lost in the twisted hair, and the hair falling
loose.

And she meets me with a slender waist, thin as the twisted
leathern nose-rein of a camel.
Her form is like the stem of a palm-tree bending over from the
weight of its fruit.

In the morning, when she wakes, the particles of musk are
lying over her bed.
She sleeps much in the morning; she does not need to gird her
waist with a working dress.

She gives with thin fingers, not thick, as if they were the
worms of the desert of Zabi,
In the evening she brightens the darkness, as if she were the
light-tower of a monk.

Toward one like her, the wise man gazes incessantly, lovingly.
She is well proportioned in height between the wearer of a
long dress and of a short frock.

The follies of men cease with youth, but my heart does not
cease to love you.
Many bitter counselors have warned me of the disaster of your
love, but I turned away from them.

Many a night has let down its curtains around me amid deep
grief,
It has whelmed me as a wave of the sea to try me with sorrow.

Then I said to the night, as slowly his huge bulk passed over
me,
As his breast, his loins, his buttocks weighed on me and then
passed afar,

" Oh long night, dawn will come, but will be no brighter without my love.
You are a wonder, with stars held up as by ropes of hemp to a
solid rock."

At other times, I have filled a leather water-bag of my people
and entered the desert,
And trod its empty wastes while the wolf howled like a gam-
bler whose family starves.

I said to the wolf, " You gather as little wealth, as little pros-
perity as I.
What either of us gains he gives away. So do we remain
thin."

Early in the morning, while the birds were still nesting, I
mounted my steed.
Well-bred was he, long-bodied, outstripping the wild beasts in
speed,

Swift to attack, to flee, to turn, yet firm as a rock swept down
by the torrent,
Bay-colored, and so smooth the saddle slips from him, as the
rain from a smooth stone,

Thin but full of life, fire boils within him like the snorting of
  a boiling kettle;
He continues at full gallop when other horses are dragging
  their feet in the dust for weariness.

A boy would be blown from his back, and even the strong rider
  loses his garments.
Fast is my steed as a top when a child has spun it well.

He has the flanks of a buck, the legs of an ostrich, and the gallop of a wolf.
From behind, his thick tail hides the space between his thighs,
  and almost sweeps the ground.

When he stands before the house, his back looks like the huge
  grinding-stone there.
The blood of many leaders of herds is in him, thick as the
  juice of henna in combed white hair.

As I rode him we saw a flock of wild sheep, the ewes like
  maidens in long-trailing robes;
They turned for flight, but already he had passed the leaders
  before they could scatter.

He outran a bull and a cow and killed them both, and they
  were made ready for cooking;
Yet he did not even sweat so as to need washing.

We returned at evening, and the eye could scarcely realize his
  beauty
For, when gazing at one part, the eye was drawn away by the
  perfection of another part.

He stood all night with his saddle and bridle on him,
He stood all night while I gazed at him admiring, and did not
  rest in his stable.

But come, my friends, as we stand here mourning, do you see
  the lightning?

See its glittering, like the flash of two moving hands, amid the
thick gathering clouds.

Its glory shines like the lamps of a monk when he has dipped
their wicks thick in oil.
I sat down with my companions and watched the lightning
and the coming storm.

So wide-spread was the rain that its right end seemed over
Quatan,
Yet we could see its left end pouring down on Satar, and
beyond that over Yazbul.

So mighty was the storm that it hurled upon their faces the
huge kanahbul trees,
The spray of it drove the wild goats down from the hills of
Quanan.

In the gardens of Taimaa not a date-tree was left standing,
Nor a building, except those strengthened with heavy stones.

The mountain, at the first downpour of the rain, looked like a
giant of our people draped in a striped cloak.
The peak of Mujaimir in the flood and rush of débris looked
like a whirling spindle.

The clouds poured forth their gift on the desert of Ghabeet,
till it blossomed
As though a Yemani merchant were spreading out all the rich
clothes from his trunks,

As though the little birds of the valley of Jiwaa awakened in
the morning
And burst forth in song after a morning draught of old, pure,
spiced wine.

As though all the wild beasts had been covered with sand and
mud, like the onion's root-bulbs.
They were drowned and lost in the depths of the desert at
evening.

THE POEM OF ANTAR [1]

Have the poets left in the garment a place for a patch to be patched by me; and did you know the abode of your beloved after reflection? [2]

The vestige of the house, which did not speak, confounded thee, until it spoke by means of signs, like one deaf and dumb.

Verily, I kept my she-camel there long grumbling, with a yearning at the blackened stones, keeping and standing firm in their own places.

It is the abode of a friend, languishing in her glance, submissive in the embrace, pleasant of smile.

Oh house of 'Ablah situated at Jiwaa, talk with me about those who resided in you. Good morning to you, O house of 'Ablah, and be safe from ruin.

I halted my she-camel in that place; and it was as though she were a high palace; in order that I might perform the wont of the lingerer.

And 'Ablah takes up her abode at Jiwaa; while our people went to Hazan, then to Mutathallam.

She took up her abode in the land of my enemies; so it became difficult for me to seek you, O daughter of Mahzam.

I was enamored of her unawares, at a time when I was killing her people, desiring her in marriage; but by your father's life I swear, this was not the time for desiring. [3]

And verily you have occupied in my heart the place of the honored loved one, so do not think otherwise than this, that you are my beloved.

And how may be the visiting of her, while her people have

[1] This is the Antar, or Antarah, who became the most noted of Arab heroes of romance.

[2] That is, have the poets left any deficiency to be supplied? Have the poets of the former days left any poetry unsaid that the poets of the present day may say it?

[3] When there was war between the two tribes, there was little use his wishing to marry her.

taken up their residence in the spring at 'Unaizatain and our people at Ghailam?

I knew that you had intended departing, for, verily, your camels were bridled on a dark night.

Nothing caused me fear of her departure, except that the baggage camels of her people were eating the seeds of the Khimkhim tree throughout the country.[4]

Amongst them were two and forty milk-giving camels, black as the wing-feathers of black crows.

When she captivates you with a mouth possessing sharp, and white teeth, sweet as to its place of kissing, delicious of taste.

As if she sees with the two eyes of a young, grown up gazelle from the deer.

It was as though the musk bag of a merchant in his case of perfumes preceded her teeth toward you from her mouth.

Or as if it is an old wine-skin, from Azri'at, preserved long, such as the kings of Rome preserve;

Or her mouth is as an ungrazed meadow, whose herbage the rain has guaranteed, in which there is but little dung; and which is not marked with the feet of animals.

The first pure showers of every rain-cloud rained upon it, and left every puddle in it bright and round like a dirham;

Sprinkling and pouring; so that the water flows upon it every evening, and is not cut off from it.

The fly enjoyed yet alone, and so it did not cease humming, as is the act of the singing drunkard;

Humming, while he rubs one foreleg against the other, as the striking on the flint of one, bent on the flint, and cut off as to his palm.

She passes her evenings and her mornings on the surface of a well-stuffed couch, while I pass my nights on the back of a bridled black horse.

And my couch is a saddle upon a horse big-boned in the leg, big in his flanks, great of girth.

Would a Shadanian she-camel cause me to arrive at her

[4] He knew that her tribe would have to move on, as there was no forage left for their camels.

abode, who is cursed with an udder scanty of milk and cut off ? [5]

After traveling all night, she is lashing her sides with her tail, and is strutting proudly, and she breaks up the mounds of earth she passes over with her foot with its sole, treading hard.

As if I in the evening am breaking the mounds of earth by means of an ostrich, very small as to the distance between its two feet, and earless. [6]

The young ostriches flock toward him, as the herds of Yamanian camels flock to a barbarous, unintelligible speaker.

They follow the crest of his head, as though it was a howdah on a large litter, tented for them.

He is small headed, who returns constantly to look after his eggs at Zil-'Ushairah; he is like a slave, with a long fur cloak and without ears.

She drank of the water of Duhruzain and then turned away, being disgusted, from the pools of stagnant water. [7]

And she swerves away with her right side from the fear of one, whistling in the evening, a big, ugly-headed one; [8]

From the fear of a cat, led at her side, every time she turned toward him in anger, he met her with both claws and mouth.

She knelt down at the edge of the pool of Rada', and groaned as though she had knelt on a reed, broken, and emitting a cracking noise.

And the sweat on the back was as though it were oil or thick pitch, with which fire is lighted round the sides of a retort.

Her places of flexure were wetted with it and she lavishly poured of it, on a spreading forelock, short and well-bred.

The length of the journey left her a strong, well-built body, like a high palace, built with cement, and rising high; and feet like the supports of a firmly pitched tent.

[5] A she-camel, upon whom this operation has been performed, is swifter, stronger, and fatter than others.

[6] He compares the fleetness of the camel to that of an ostrich.

[7] Referring to the she-camel.

[8] The big, ugly-headed one is the whip with its heavy handle, or a cat.

And surely I recollected you, even when the lances were drinking my blood, and bright swords of Indian make were dripping with my blood.

I wished to kiss the swords, for verily they shone as bright as the flash of the foretooth of your smiling mouth.

If you lower your veil over yourself in front of me, of what use will it be? for, verily, I am expert in capturing the mailed horseman.

Praise me for the qualities which you know I possess, for, verily, when I am not ill-treated, I am gentle to associate with.

And if I am ill-treated, then, verily, my tyranny is severe, very bitter is the taste of it, as the taste of the colocynth.

And, verily, I have drunk wine after the midday heats have subsided, buying it with the bright stamped coin.

From a glass, yellow with the lines of the glass-cutter on it, which was accompanied by a white-stoppered bottle on the left-hand side.

And when I have drunk, verily, I am the squanderer of my property, and my honor is great, and is not sullied.[9]

And when I have become sober, I do not diminish in my generosity, and as you know, so are my qualities and my liberality.

And many a husband of a beautiful woman, I have left prostrate on the ground, with his shoulders hissing like the side of the mouth of one with a split lip.[10]

My two hands preceded him with a hasty blow, striking him before he could strike me; and with the drops of blood from a penetrating stroke, red like the color of Brazil wood.

Why did you not ask the horsemen, O daughter Malik! if you were ignorant, concerning what you did not know about my condition,

At a time when I never ceased to be in the saddle of a long striding, wounded, sturdy horse, against whom the warriors came in succession.

[9] That is, drunkenness makes him generous and not ill-tempered. The Arabs, before Mohammed, considered drinking with one's friends to show a generous disposition.

[10] That is, the blood was spurting and hissing from a wound in his shoulder.

At one time he is detached to charge the enemy with the lance, and at another he joins the large host with their bows tightly strung.

He who was present in the battle will inform you that verily I rush into battle, but I abstain at the time of taking the booty.

I see spoils, which, if I want I would win; but my bashfulness and my magnanimity hold me back from them.

And many a fully armed one, whom the warriors shunned fighting with, neither a hastener in flight, nor a surrenderer;

My hands were generous to him by a quick point with a straightened spear, strong in the joints;

Inflicting a wound wide of its two sides, the sound of the flow of blood from it leads at night the prowling wolves, burning with hunger.

I rent his vesture with a rigid spear, for the noble one is not forbidden to the spears.

Then I left him a prey for the wild beasts, who seize him, and gnaw the beauty of his fingers and wrist.

And many a long, closely woven coat of mail, I have split open the links of it, with a sword, off one defending his rights, and renowned for bravery.

Whose hands are ready with gambling arrows when it is winter, a tearer-down of the signs of the wine-sellers, and one reproached for his extravagance.[11]

When he saw that I had descended from my horse and was intending killing him, he showed his teeth, but without smiling.[12]

My meeting with him was when the day spread out, and he was as if his fingers and his head were dyed with indigo.[13]

I pierced him with my spear, and then I set upon him with my Indian sword pure of steel, and keen.

A warrior, so stately in size as if his clothes were on a high

[11] The richer Arabs gamble as to who shall kill his camel in the time of scarcity to distribute the flesh amongst the poor. The wine-sellers take down their signs when they have run out of liquor; the meaning of tearing down the signs being that he drinks up all their wine.

[12] The allusion is to the poet's killing Zamzam, father of Husain and Harim, who insulted him. See close of the poem.

[13] The dried blood was of an indigo color.

tree: soft leather shoes are worn by him and he is not twinned.

Oh, how wonderful is the beauty of the doe of the hunt, to whom is she lawful? To me she is unlawful; would to God that she was not unlawful.[14]

So, I sent my female slave, and said to her, " Go, find out news of her and inform me."

She said, " I saw carelessness on the part of the enemies, and that the doe is possible to him who is shooting."

And it was as though she looked toward me with the neck of a doe, a fawn of the gazelles, pure and with a white upper lip.

I am informed that 'Amru is unthankful for my kindness while ingratitude is a cause of evil to the soul of the giver.[15]

And, verily, I remember the advice of my uncle, in the battle, when the two lips quiver from off the white teeth of the mouth,

In the thick of the battle, of which the warriors do not complain of the rigors, except with an unintelligible noise.

When they (i.e., my people) defended themselves with me against the spears of the enemy, I did not refrain from them (i.e., the spears) through cowardice, but the place of my advance had become too strait.

When I heard the cry of Murrah rise, and saw the two sons of Rabi'ah in the thick dust,

While the tribe of Muhallam were struggling under their banners, and death was under the banners of the tribe of Mulhallam,

I made sure that at the time of their encounter there would be a blow, which would make the heads fly from the bodies, as the bird flies from off her young ones sitting close.

When I saw the people, while their mass advanced, excite one another to fight, I turned against them without being reproached for any want of bravery.

They were calling 'Antarah, while the spears were as though they were well-ropes in the breast of Adham.

---

[14] Here he again reverts to address his sweetheart. The Arabs may not marry with a woman of a tribe with whom they are at war.

[15] 'Amru, the 'Absian, who insulted the poet.

They were calling 'Antarah, while the swords were as though they were the flash of lightnings in a dark cloud.

They were calling 'Antarah, while the arrows were flying, as though they were a flight of locusts, hovering above watering places.

They were calling " O 'Antarah," while the coats of mail shone with close rings, shining as though they were the eyeballs of frogs floating in a wavy pond.

I did not cease charging them, (the enemy,) with the prominent part of his (horse's) throat and breast, until he became covered with a shirt of blood.

Then he turned on account of the falling of the spears on his breast, and complained to me with tears and whinnyings.

If he had known what conversation was, he would have complained with words, and verily he would have, had he known speech, talked with me.

And verily the speech of the horsemen, " Woe to you, 'Antarah, advance, and attack the enemy," cured my soul and removed its sickness.

While the horses sternly frowning were charging over the soft soil, being partly the long-bodied mares, and partly the long-bodied, well-bred horses.

My riding-camels are tractable, they go wherever I wish; while my intellect is my helper, and I drive it forward with a firm order.[16]

Verily, it lay beyond my power that I should visit you; so, know what you have known, and some of what you have not known.

The lances of the tribe of Bagheez intercepted you and the perpetrators of the war set aside those who did not perpetrate it.

And, verily, I turned the horse for the attack, while his neck was bleeding, until the horses began to shun me.

And verily I feared that I should die, while there has not yet been a turn for war against the two sons of Zamzam; [17]

---

[16] That is, I carry out my plans with sagacity and determination.

[17] I feared that I should die, before I had fought the two sons of Zamzam. 'Antarah killed their father during the war between the tribes

The two revilers of my honor, while I did not revile them, and the threateners of my blood, when I did not see them.

There is no wonder should they do so, for I left their father a prey for the wild beasts and every large old vulture.

of 'Abs and Fazárah, wherein the latter were defeated with great loss. Harim and Husain, the two sons of Zamzam, were killed shortly afterward.

THE POEM OF ZUHAIR [1]

"Does the blackened ruin, situated in the stony ground between Durraj and Mutathallam, which did not speak to me, when addressed, belong to the abode of Ummi Awfa?

"And is it her dwelling at the two stony meadows, seeming as though they were the renewed tattoo marks in the sinews of the wrist?

"The wild cows and the white deer are wandering about there, one herd behind the other, while their young are springing up from every lying-down place.

"I stood again near it, (the encampment of the tribe of Awfa,) after an absence of twenty years, and with some efforts, I know her abode again after thinking awhile.

"I recognized the three stones blackened by fire at the place where the kettle used to be placed at night, and the trench round the encampment, which had not burst, like the source of a pool.

"And when I recognized the encampment I said to its site, 'Now good morning, oh spot; may you be safe from dangers.'

"Look, oh my friend! do you see any women traveling on camels, going over the high ground above the stream of Jurthum? [2]

"They have covered their howdahs with coverlets of high value, and with a thin screen, the fringes of which are red, resembling blood.

"And they inclined toward the valley of Soobán, ascending the center of it, and in their faces were the fascinating

[1] This poem begins, as do most Arab poems, with love longings, but soon drifts into praise of two peacemakers and the story of the feud between two tribes which preceded the peace. From this field the poem soon wanders to the philosophic maxims of the author. Zuhair is above all a philosopher.

[2] He fancies he sees the women again whom he saw twenty years previously, and he appeals to his companion to know if what he sees is real.

looks of a soft-bodied person brought up in easy circumstances.

"They arose early in the morning and got up at dawn, and they went straight to the valley of Rass as the hand goes unswervingly to the mouth, when eating.

"And amongst them is a place of amusement for the far-sighted one, and a pleasant sight for the eye of the looker who looks attentively.

"As if the pieces of dyed wool which they left in every place in which they halted, were the seeds of night-shade which have not been crushed.

"When they arrived at the water, the mass of which was blue from intense purity, they laid down their walking sticks, (*i.e.,* took their lodging there,) like the dweller who has pitched his tents.

"They kept the hill of Qanan and the rough ground about it on their hand; while there are many, dwelling in Qanan, the shedding of whose blood is lawful and unlawful.[3]

"They came out from the valley of Soobán, then they crossed it, riding in every Qainian howdah new and widened.

"Then I swear by the temple, round which walk the men who built it from the tribes of Quraish and Jurhum.[4]

"An oath, that you are verily two excellent chiefs, who are found worthy of honor in every condition, between ease and distress.[5]

"The two endeavorers from the tribe of Ghaiz bin Murrah strove in making peace after the connection between the tribes had become broken, on account of the shedding of blood.

"You repaired with peace the condition of the tribes of 'Abs and Zubyán, after they had fought with one another, and ground up the perfume of Manshim between them.[6]

---

[3] There are many enemies and many friends dwelling there.

[4] This refers to the temple at Mecca which was built by Ismail, son of Abraham, ancestor of the tribe of Quraish, who married a woman of Jurhum, an old tribe of Yaman, who were the keepers of the temple before Quraish.

[5] The theme changes here abruptly, to praise of two peacemakers.

[6] Some Arabs, making a league to be revenged against their enemies,

" And indeed you said, ' if we bring about peace perfectly by the spending of money and the conferring of benefits, and by good words, we shall be safe from the danger of the two tribes, destroying each other.'

" You occupied by reason of this the best of positions, and became far from the reproach of being undutiful and sinful.

" And you became great in the high nobility of Ma'add; may you be guided in the right way; and he who spends his treasure of glory will become great.

" The memory of the wounds is obliterated by the hundreds of camels, and he, who commenced paying off the blood money by instalments, was not guilty of it (*i.e.,* of making war).

" One tribe pays it to another tribe as an indemnity, while they who gave the indemnity did not shed blood sufficient for the filling of a cupping glass.

" Then there was being driven to them from the property you inherited, a booty of various sorts from young camels with slit ears.

" Now, convey from me to the tribe of Zubyán and their allies a message,—' verily you have sworn by every sort of oath to keep the peace.'

" Do not conceal from God what is in your breast that it may be hidden; whatever is concealed, God knows all about it.

" Either it will be put off and placed recorded in a book, and preserved there until the judgment day; or the punishment be hastened and so he will take revenge.

" And war is not but what you have learnt it to be, and what you have experienced, and what is said concerning it, is not a story based on suppositions.

" When you stir it up, you will stir it up as an accursed thing, and it will become greedy when you excite its greed and it will rage fiercely.

took oath with their hands plunged in a certain perfume, made by Manshim, as a sign of their coalition. They fought until they were slain to the last of them. Hence the proverb, " More unlucky than the perfume of Manshim."

"Then it will grind you as the grinding of the upper mill-stone against the lower, and it will conceive immediately after one birth and it will produce twins.[7]

"By my life I swear, how good a tribe it is upon whom Husain Bin Zamzam brought an injury by committing a crime which did not please them.[8]

"And he had concealed his hatred, and did not display it, and did not proceed to carry out his intention until he got a good opportunity.

"And he said, 'I will perform my object of avenging my-self, and I will guard myself from my enemy with a thousand bridled horses behind me.'

"Then he attacked his victim from 'Abs, but did not cause fear to the people of the many houses, near which death had thrown down his baggage.[9]

"They allowed their animals to graze until when the inter-val between the hours of drinking was finished, they took them to the deep pool, which is divided by weapons and by shedding of blood.[10]

"They accomplished their object amongst themselves, then they led the animals back to the pasture of unwholesome in-digestible grass.

"I have grown weary of the troubles of life; and he, who lives eighty years will, mayest thou have no father if thou doubt [11] grow weary.

"And I know what has happened to-day and yesterday,

[7] The misfortunes arising from war are double.

[8] Husain Bin Zamzam's father was killed during the war between the Benî Zubyân and the Benî 'Abs. When peace was concluded be-tween the tribes, he made a vow secretly that he would kill one of the tribe of 'Abs out of the revenge for his father. This he did, but when the Benî 'Abs came to take revenge on him, Hârith Ibn 'Awf offered them one hundred camels as blood money or his own son to kill. The 'Absioms took the camels and spared his son. The poet is now prais-ing them for their act.

[9] He killed no one while the peace was in force except the one person on whom he meant to take revenge.

[10] By the deep pool is meant war, and the meaning of the lines is that the tribes refrained from war for a certain time, after which they again had recourse to arms.

[11] A common term of imprecation.

before it, but verily, of the knowledge of what will happen to-morrow; I am ignorant.

" I see death is like the blundering of a blind camel;— him whom he meets he kills, and he whom he misses lives and will become old.

" And he who does not act with kindness in many affairs will be torn by teeth and trampled under foot.

" And he, who makes benevolent acts intervene before honor, increases his honor; and he, who does not avoid abuse, will be abused.

" He, who is possessed of plenty, and is miserly with his great wealth toward his people, will be dispensed with, and abused.

" He who keeps his word, will not be reviled; and he whose heart is guided to self-satisfying benevolence will not stammer.

" And he who dreads the causes of death, they will reach him, even if he ascends the tracts of the heavens with a ladder.

" And he, who shows kindness to one not deserving it, his praise will be a reproach against him, and he will repent of having shown kindness.

" And he who rebels against the butt ends of the spears, then verily he will have to obey the spear points joined to every long spear shaft.[12]

" And he who does not repulse with his weapons from his tank, will have it broken; and he who does not oppress the people will be oppressed.

" And he who travels should consider his friend an enemy; and he who does not respect himself will not be respected.

" And he, who is always seeking to bear the burdens of other people, and does not excuse himself from it, will one day by reason of his abasement, repent.

" And whatever of character there is in a man, even though he thinks it concealed from people, it is known.

[12] The wandering desert Arabs when they met used to present the butt ends of their spears toward one another if their intentions were peaceful, the points if they intended fighting.

" He, who does not cease asking people to carry him, and does not make himself independent of them even for one day of the time, will be regarded with disgust.

" Many silent ones you see, pleasing to you, but their excess in wisdom or deficiency will appear at the time of talking.

" The tongue of a man is one half, and the other half is his mind, and here is nothing besides these two, except the shape of the blood and the flesh.

" And verily, as to the folly of an old man there is no wisdom after it, but the young man after his folly may become wise.

" We asked of you, and you gave, and we returned to the asking and you returned to the giving, and he who increases the asking, will one day be disappointed."

This is the end of this publication.

Any remaining blank pages are for our book binding
requirements and are blank on purpose.

To search thousands of interesting publications like this one,
please remember to visit our website at:

http://www.kessinger.net

CPSIA information can be obtained
at www.ICGtesting.com
Printed in the USA
BVHW022306270223
659375BV00005B/47

9 781162 860138